THE SCENT GALLERY

THE SCENT GALLERY

Christine McNeill

Shoestring Press

All rights reserved. No part of this work covered by the copyright hereon may be reproduced or used in any means – graphic, electronic, or mechanical, including copying, recording, taping, or information storage and retrieval systems – without written permission of the publisher.

Printed by imprintdigital
Upton Pyne, Exeter
www.imprintdigital.net

Typeset by narrator
www.narrator.me.uk
enquiries@narrator.me.uk

Published by Shoestring Press
19 Devonshire Avenue, Beeston, Nottingham, NG9 1BS
(0115) 925 1827
www.shoestringpress.co.uk

First published 2011
© Copyright: Christine McNeill
The moral right of the author has been asserted.
ISBN 978 1 907356 29 2

ACKNOWLEDGEMENTS

Acknowledgements are due to the following publications, where the poems, or versions of them, first appeared:

Agenda, Acumen, "Blood Line" (Anthology), Critical Quarterly, Cyphers (Ireland), Dreamcatcher, Illuminations, Magma, New Walk, New Welsh Review, Other Poetry, Planet, Poetry Ireland Review, Red Wheelbarrow, Scintilla 13, 14 + 15, Staple, Stand, The Interpreter's House.

for Anne

i.m.

Contents

An act of prayer	1
Discovery	2
Guide book	4
Diviner	5
Moving train	7
Unearthly hour	9
House	10
Confirmation	11
Release	12
Setting foot	14
Chinese lament	16
Eve	17
Water	18
Transfigured night	20
Morning's weather	21
Posing for Holbein	23
The love of art	25
Medieval lady in stained glass	27
Portfolio	28
The Scent Gallery	30
Idyll	31
Window-talk	32
Contact	34
One slow evening	35
Beggar	37
Hedy Lamarr's ashes return home	38
Confrontation	39
A gentler age	40
On the edge	41
Observing love and war	42

Tender night	43
Martha's reverie	45
Bracelet in a shoe	49
Time	50
The Anaesthetist	51
20th July 1969	53
Friday 3 p.m.	55
Praying in secret	56
Among ruins	58
Eclipsed moon	60
I became a famous artist in old age	61
Contemplation	63

AN ACT OF PRAYER

Cave-men wanting to reach
the God behind rock
and say
I'm here — take note!,

crooked their fingers
against the wall
and with mouth-paint
blew the hand's imprint
onto the stone.

The image survived
for twenty-eight thousand years,
making you wonder
whether it brought the
desired *Yes, I'm here*,

or, as the hand slipped,
an inner light
holding the dark
until taken up
by the sun outside.

If I were to do it in words,
would you receive
the sounds of my soul,
answer *I'm here*
and *You need to go it alone?*

DISCOVERY

John Stratton, Walter Grimbald, Henry Baniard –
medieval names in a calendar of Norwich deeds.
Their occupations draper, dyer, skinner –
you plod through accounts of who sold what to whom.

Scrutinise their tiny writing.
It is so big this search
for the medieval psyche –
each clue a minute's scissor-sharp bliss

before it blurs, as if in salt-wind-drizzle.
A detective without a client
you're after evidence:
names flesh out, vibrate with meaning,

turn into smiles, move forward
into other smiles that almost mock
your examining mind. Doors open
as you heap discovery upon discovery,

back home scrape dirt off excavated
stained glass, guiding the blade
so as not to harm the emerging image.
Rinsing the find, you hold it up:

the serrated edge of a leaf,
contours of a saint's robe.
Did *Henry Baniard* donate this glass
to the church in thanksgiving

for the birth of a son?
Arm raised into the light
your lips move:
but there's nothing for words to land on.

GUIDE BOOK

> *"In reading, like dreaming,*
> *one enters a different world ..."* – Richard Benz

Nothing pleads between pages –
only an insect-smudge – a mayfly.

That feeling, as you begin to read,
like others before you coming to the same pool to drink.

In the Middle Ages on Christmas Eve
the church was aglow with dripping candles.

Herbs were strewn on the aisle
to drive out sickness and death.

Evenings, when the faithful emerged
after giving thanks for a good harvest,

they looked at the New Moon,
hoping it could lift them into God's hands.

You touch the poppy-heads on pews
worn down by the palms of believers

who drew the wood into their praying spell.
As a boy in short trousers and knee-socks

on icy mornings,
you pulled the bell rope with all your strength,

as if pulling down God;
sank to the cold slabs,

and were lifted higher and higher,
face borrowing from the dark of the church.

DIVINER

His work took him over fields
searching the ploughed earth
for what it had thrown up.

Sometimes the land dozed in sunshine
and a calm entered his spirits,
affirming who he was.

Other times, pleading for inner guidance,
he watched a sparrow-hawk skirting a copse,
argued with himself about the right and wrong

of going forward into the past.
Walked back the long way into evening,
the moon's cap of light

tumbled into puddles,
a wandering scent
preyed on his mind.

But when finding the remains
of crockery, or a piece of medieval glass,
making out the drawing of a lion's head,

an oak leaf or a pointing finger,
he joyfully began a step by step conjecture:
date, location, circumstance.

Then the field was like a whole
ancient village buzzing with people;
he held each fragment up to the light:

the precious *fruit* the earth had grown;
a mystery that passed over deep furrows
to which he belonged.

MOVING TRAIN

He'd wanted pictures taken
of his last holiday in the Austrian Alps.
Studied them afterwards, noting
the black dot of an eagle in the blue sky
that had escaped us. We zoomed in on his
leaning more heavily on the walking-stick,
looking, not at the camera, but into the distance.

Leobersdorf, Bad Vöslau, Wiener Neustadt,
he wrote down the passing train-stations.
Was it to make the strangeness lying beyond
his terminal illness more familiar to himself?
He doubled the number of stops,
added fourteen, halved the total,
took off the original figure that left him with *seven*.

There're seven trees in his garden.
One, whose scarlet berries he called
my mermaid gems, we prune.
I hook down a branch
with his walking-stick.
While you saw
I almost hang in the air

trying to keep the branch low,
feeling as if my head were taking off
into that blue beyond the withering leaves
to follow his name-tape on the stick.
As you cut into the wood
I feel my strength ebb,
call out *Stop!*

and we both let go.
Catching your breath
you kiss me:
the wind blows the sensation up through the leaves
to where we can't follow,
but imagine it blend into the many unseen things
of which at this moment we are certain.

UNEARTHLY HOUR

Alone on the station platform
with trains coming and going
you wanted to end your young life
that seemed without hope.

Time passed. Nothing happened
except the certainty
that you would throw yourself
onto the track.

A hand on your shoulder:
Is something wrong?
An old lady
at this unearthly hour.

No, you replied. Enough
to break your death wish
as calmly you watched the stranger
get on the next train.

Your cat sat by the door.
Ear-tips translucent in the light
you'd left burning
into your story

whose impact was absorbed
by the ticking clock.
The cat drank up the silence.
Alert to your coming home.

HOUSE

When small, I made one with plastic cubes.
Later, dad showed me how to put one up with cards.
Now my house is fifteen metres away from collapse.

Mother pushed me in the pram
to the edge of the cliff. Here I said my first word.
Her father had built the house brick by brick.

When I contemplate the horizon
it doesn't matter that where I live
can't be insured, and when it falls

there won't be compensation.
The spot was chosen
so that we got used to infinity.

The cliff has slipped.
Each morning I pace the garden
to measure how much is left.

At ten metres the house will be demolished.
The tulips I bought in the depth of winter:
a vibrant red that drew everything

second-hand into their spell.
Within three days the flowers withered,
but petals, leaves, and pollen remained.

Now in a gale when windows shake
I think of the tulips' shrivelled shell:
how somewhere within life held.

CONFIRMATION

After receiving communion,
confirmation and blessing,
tasting for the first time the sacred,

at grandma's home you're given the task
of dusting her favourite porcelain:
a girl with harp, a prince on horseback …

You put each figurine
carefully back in place,
smelling grandma's rosewater-scent.

Years later, wheeling your mother
around the city's shop-windows,
you stopped before a display of *Meissen*:

cups and saucers surrounded by rose-petals:
suddenly their deep-passion scent
came through the glass.

You encountered it again
on a plane flying over a world of clouds
pouring in with a rush of feelings

as you recalled walking in your black suit
over fresh snow, smelling that rose-scent
knowing snow had no scent at all.

RELEASE

We distributed linen to holiday flats.
My life broken, she said, cheek bruised
by her husband's hand.

One afternoon I took her to an artist's studio:
wooden spoon, spatula, whisk
wilfully deformed, wrapped in silk.

She asked the artist the meaning.
He pointed at a bent knife:
A dialogue between denaturalised objects.

She didn't understand.
Brought from India
to enter an arranged marriage,

she struggled with English:
too slow with cooking and cleaning,
her husband's job on the line,

he frequently hit her.
She longed to go back to her dad.
I touched her scarred cheek:

You must leave.
She took my side of the sheet,
swiftly folded it herself.

One day we walked through fields
by a huge forest.
There was weather in her closed fist

as she made breathless strides
towards a patch of wild orchids:
their petals like dripping wax

etched with fine purple brushstrokes.
They spoke of courage,
dignity and grace.

Then a sudden gust of wind shook the trees
as if to tear out all their secrets.
And rain came down in sheets.

Later in her kitchen, gazing at the rain,
she reached for a plant on the windowsill
that was lacking light: cupped it in both hands and cried.

SETTING FOOT

You never discovered the reason
they broke down the door
in your homeland,

smashing your possessions,
but you assumed it had to do
with your faith.

You decided to leave.
Kissed your father's forehead
as if going for a stroll,

walked down the rough track
and on seeing a drop of dew
paused.

The mysterious broke in:
the sun rising, primordial half-bloom,
and you standing with the whole family, in awe.

Watching that drop of dew,
you wanted to stay,
and were desperate to go.

I think of this as I enter my father's house
for the last time. Furniture and wall-hangings
have gone. Broken wood bundled,

ornaments of no use bagged.
The harvest is over, he would have said.
I wonder who the rooms will please next.

Difficult to imagine renewal
when memories crash in
like giant rocks. A flight of birds

as years ago we stood,
father and I,
gazing at the full moon:

the stillness broken
by the beating of wings overhead
as if air were communing with earth.

My thoughts drifted to you,
setting foot in this country,
going through *Nothing to Declare*

when father stepped back into the house.

CHINESE LAMENT

Ki Chuen takes communion
in Beijing's Catholic church
where the priest is accountable to the state.

Ki Chuen receives his god in cupped hands.
Bites and chews. His god
travels down the digestive tract.

On icons this god shows no blood.
Perched on the lap of a manly Virgin
he raises a finger.

Ki Chuen chops up his lunch.
Two hundred miles away
the land of his ancestors was taken by the government.

He eats slowly, so as not to disturb
the swallowed god.
His guts like snakes asleep in deep undergrowth.

EVE

You cry out in your sleep –
a sound like a child's dismay –
I right your pillow,

and when you continue that cry
I let my hand glide inches above
your face

before allowing it to meet
your mouth

that does not want
to draw close
to my smiling one.

You in your sleep,
I in my play
seem to perish in distance –

Darling, I peeled all the apples
in the store-cupboard,

with a deer bone
brought your hunting boots
to a blazing shine

and now welcome you
to a home deeper
than where you find yourself –

with all my might
press down on you

the knowledge you don't want me to have.

WATER

    i. m. Brigitte S.

It's raining as I enter the pool, part the water
so I can lie flat,
and keep on parting it, feet drawing in and out
so I can move ahead.

You let yourself fall
into the river, polluted like your drugged body –
there was no sunlight
laughing under your belly.

Your tongue was lead. The sounds of the current
like cracking eggs. Words still in your head
bounced away
never to be retrieved.

Your ending absorbs my brain
as I offer each stroke back to the water:
if something of me could heal you now,
could turn your death into life?

With each thought lift you from the river,
your arms not limp, not holding a posy
of blood-red flowers as in my dream,
but open to catch a ball

and throw it back, laughing at my
missing it: the sun teasing your neck
while I swim another lap, feeling the
underwater breeze: Look –

I'm making love to every ripple,
like a swan extract food from the deep:
sun like a crystal –
in the blue sky a gull writes its signature.

TRANSFIGURED NIGHT

Your tongue encircles mine
like carving something wicked
from my heart.

On a picture postcard
I see a mass of black heat
tumbling over the brow of a hill,

whipping up stones,
uprooting trees –
the lava's consuming mouth.

You look at my face.
Why did you stop?
Afraid passion could turn to violence?

In the War my granny,
seeing an ox-tongue in a butcher's window,
not having the money,

imagined being a fly
feasting on the meat.
It didn't stop her hunger.

Later she talked about Korean Pansori singers
only perfecting their voices in old age
when loneliness and death unite on their tongues.

You lead me into the shower.
In the gentle waterfall my birdlike neck
unwinds a narrative your tongue laps up.

MORNING'S WEATHER

Sunlight creeps through the net curtains
as your car slides out of the driveway
and in an instant you are off my visual map.

Clouds spill over the sun, but a watery ray
manages to light up the drawing of an embrace.

Wind begins to get trees into gentle gymnastics
when you walk back in
having lost the car-key after parking in town,

caught a train home to fetch the reserve one.
You rush out the door,

and as I listen to the train
passing the bottom of our garden,
light, sharp as a glacier, streams over the drawing

of a black slave
held in the arms of his white-robed master.

I shake loose the pyjama sleeves,
fold them on top of the trousers
under the pillow.

In the next room, a violin
rises and falls,

dances around a particular chord,
encourages it to climb higher
and boldly stand like an emperor

on a sunlit terrace.
Dances around the next rise and fall;

and plumping up pillows
I see a jay on the bare cotoneaster,
eyes closed, as if fallen asleep

while preening.
The melody leaps

and I'm in the heart of it:
in the heart of curtains shifting in the wind,
in the jay blinking at a rush of clouds –

when the final chord fades,
the curtains still, the jay gone,
there's the beauty of a made bed.

POSING FOR HOLBEIN

(after "Lady with a Squirrel and a Starling")

The movements of his brush fill me
with longing; a chained squirrel on my lap
cracking a nut – symbol for the child I birthed.

I finger the chain as if praying the rosary,
reading the Lord's wisdom in every bead.
He paints a starling on a fig branch,

a pun on East Harling where I live.
Adjusts the translucent garment on my chest –
my flesh exposed

as if to whispering grass.
I say the name of my child. Think of spring
when instead of the sky

white apple-blossom holds divinity.
Rumour is spreading the king has an eye
on the young Anne Boleyn: trying for an heir –

a mystery I have achieved.
Holbein studies my face.
This is how pure loneliness gets:

as if an angel makes me look
at the aching immensity of space.
I miss my son. They say *loving*

is an art. I pray for evening to come.
For him to be taken from the wet-nurse
to lie at peace in my arms.

He asks me to look
at the rain on the window.
My thoughts net its steady fall.

I wish his brush could fill me
like sunlight a leaf. Could teach me
the art of being alone.

THE LOVE OF ART

Circling like a cat looking for
its customary resting-place,
compass-needle of a cigarette
tilting from the corner of your mouth,
you rage at your blindness.

But when in the rocking-chair
examining a painting,
propping the peacock-patterned cushion
high against your back,

when told size and subject,
your hand glides mercurially –
waits for that invisible spark
that makes you say: *I like it –*
will try to sell it in my gallery.

So hard to define how paint unseen
can form a mental picture.
'Grant me a little longer,' you quote Rilke,
'I want to love it like no other.'

It is love you're waiting for,
as fingertips, tapping the texture,
walk on feelings

before the intellect intrudes
and you inwardly argue
about the validity of intuition

until, in your shadowed vision,
you glimpse something akin to a mirage,
are almost moved to tears:

This is art, you say.

It is then that you,
the painting and the room
transmit an energy
and shimmer –

before a frown sets in:
I'm not sure at all.
Smiling, you add: *Who is?*

MEDIEVAL LADY IN STAINED GLASS

Startled by the roving beam of his torch,
silverfish flick into the lead above my crown.
His eager gaze swoops me up
and sets me down.
A noble woman of Dutch origin, I was the wife
of a Cornish duke in the service of the king.
He searches for proof that I'd been
painted in England, is so close to my blue robe
that in his eyes I read the love I had
for bluebell woods, for twisty lanes,
for hills like fine fur.

After my husband's death, trees paled,
rivers wound emptily from source to mouth.
The voice in me that knew what loving had once meant
could not tolerate the nothingness,
and soon sleep opened into infinity.

Beside me, The Virgin listens to the maker of the night,
while he talks to me, his age justifying
itself to my youth. Not that he knows more
but differently: who painted me,
the Jacobi process used in repairing my panel.

When at the end of the day darkness
makes him draw away, he does so
with an air of satisfaction
as though he succeeded
in undressing me.

PORTFOLIO

Between us were thirty years and a passion
for art. The younger, you held forth
about Tracy Emin, Damien Hirst.
I was tuned in to the Impressionists –
colour, tranquillity, above self-promotion.
Like Picasso you could make
a bull's head from driftwood and iron bar.
Evenings you walked in drunk
but with a charm that sparked our verbal exchanges,
and in the core of what we discussed
lay the mutual recognition of each other's
                                                  loneliness.

That is love, you said,
squeezing the glass in your hand so tight,
it cracked. Blood mingled with whisky.
By the fence, in dusk,
a deer stood stock-still.
Then sprinted into the woods beyond.

The portfolio I discovered after your death.
You'd drunk yourself to the grave.
An oddball, who couldn't make it in life.
If death is terrible,
then better be done with it now, you said,
if it is sweet,
all the more reason to welcome it.

At our last talk midges swarmed
around your thin arms.
The agave you'd pinched
from a public display and planted in my pot
was bursting with health.
With some strange instrument

you burnt the shape of a human figure
onto a sycamore leaf,
thanked me for having cooked
your favourite meal.

Now the rocking-chair
speaks the only language I know.

I reach for the red ribbon
on your portfolio: with a gentle tug
it would fall open, disclosing sheets of drawings;

but my finger only hovers inside the loop;
plays with the notion of the linear
arrested for good.

THE SCENT GALLERY

They know that *surrender* smells
of citrus fruit. Burned as incense
when the flag was raised,
its smoke signalled to the enemy.

They know the scent of a medieval maid:
her poverty, the soreness of drudgery;
a decomposed raven poulticed
to bring her calm at the end of day.

But how do they know the scent of the sun
to bottle it up and release in a gallery?
Is it a phantom vanilla warming the nostrils –
what is the perfume of intense heat?

I know the scent of snow in mid-summer:
time stripped like a daisy in *He loves me/*
he loves me not. A massive stroke
and in your lifelessness summer burst –

snow sealed off all living,
the knife-edge cold slicing the throat,
a wild tang, and a cricket chirred
at the other side of the garden

when the postman delivered a letter
from your Vietnamese sponsored child
who'd written he liked the song of cicadas
and that he could smell *love* in a green field.

IDYLL

We counted four cygnets beside their parents,
dipping small grey heads
into the lake – the adults
showing what food to extract.

Then another head popped up – five –
and was gone. We, on the shore,
entranced by this *en famille*,
looked on while songbirds wove trees

and sky into acoustic delight.
Then there were six: precise as
commas risen to the surface of the lake.
We linked arms;

our hair and skin passed along
sun-dappled leaves,
and lying down, we were a still wave
covering fungi, grasses, empty snail shells.

WINDOW-TALK

She was not one for singing in the bath,
but when the mood took her, opened
the window and threw out words
like silk scarves – anything that welled up
from the unconscious: love words,
swear words, words she'd never dared
to think, and those someone else
might have uttered, floated into the air.

She spoke in a general's voice,
as a young girl pleading to be heard,
or a father condemning
what he could not possess.
Over the lumps of trees
they came back as lions or lambs, and she
pressed a towel to her lips – the ritual
of curtaining her inner self.

Once, she read of the Renaissance theory
that an image could travel through air,
repeatedly produce a likeness of itself
before it reached the eye of the beholder.
Her voice stepped out into an albino sun,
plosives falling like petals.
It's up to you, she said,

and a voice in her head countered
I've just thought the same.
She faltered. Which thought had been hers?
Birds swooped from trees on her bangled arms.
Swaying her hips, she began to sing,
believing that what she was thinking
would fit anyone's hand.

CONTACT

Removing a feather
from the inner lining
of the jacket she'd worn
in the Himalayas

he took a photo of it,
enlarged the negative,
hung it over his bed.

The wispy strand resembled
a female body at rest:

as she, after a bath

and he
touching the cool window-pane
with a moist hand

so that rivulets ran
beneath his fingers

to where a shower of meteorites
fell to earth

where snow
blanketed her body –
whiteness continuously
renewing itself

where ice
kept bones and skin intact

to where not even his longing
could meet her distance, her fall.

ONE SLOW EVENING

I need fresh air I said, and closed the door.
My husband shredded our argument on the hotel's
double-bed, lit cigarette after cigarette –
a September night, I wore a summer skirt –
how long is an hour?

Approaching from behind, they asked me the time.
When the knife was at my throat,
my mind became like wood.
They pinned back my arms,
frogmarched me onto a tow-path,

ripped off my skirt - their hands still children's
but in their frenzy savage claws;
they punched and kicked; knew
what fists could do, had seen
their mothers on all fours from a blow.

One of those mothers praises Bible-study
and her two sons born on foreign soil,
somersaulting off the back of a van,
landing with cocky grins among indigenous boys
who sneered at their out-of-fashion clothes.

I look at her in the witness-box, and remember
the word *bitch* criss-crossing my skin,
flattening it into powder, into ash flicked from a cigarette –
the cold water of a stinking canal
closing over my heart.

Somebody saw my thrashing arms –
not my husband, who understood so well,
made cups of tea, *but now it's all over, darling.*
His hand on my lap –
Look at me!

I did, and saw tumbling graves
where one slow evening
peeling an orange in a sea of nettles
the juice ran to its death
before it reached my mouth,

the dipping sun melted a stained-glass saint,
and in a nearby field a cow
licked a bull's penis; her long tongue
charted him tenderly,
while gnats bit my bare arms.

BEGGAR

Halfway down the underground
she squats, palm up,
leather jacket bought from six months' alms.

Her four-year old beside her,
mid-morning she walks him in the park.
Finds drug needles, discarded condoms.

A ghost comes to haunt:
an old woman she'd threatened,
fled with her purse, was never caught.

At the supermarket the check-out lad
called by another *Spotty face*,
scanning her groceries, makes a mistake.

Her little boy asks: *Where do words go?*
From somewhere deep, she answers:
When they've used up all their power

they dissolve. This resurrects the lad.
Mistake deleted, the till opens.
She pays. The other lad stands cockily

at the exit. Their eyes meet.
Forgive me hangs on her lips
until she's back underground.

HEDY LAMARR'S ASHES RETURN HOME

My parents assuaged hunger with gossip. The chainsaw
of *ch's*, extra breath for tyrannical plosives.

In the communal kitchen they chopped up daily events
amid shouts and commands.

In the dining-room there was silence
as a plate of fried brawn was wolfed down.

In the bedroom they made-believe
with vowels turning transvestite.

Swallowing my Viennese accent, changing my name,
I went off to Hollywood to become a star.

In my salon, I got rid of adjectival phrases
still in my system, designed complex machinery.

Now I'm shown my humble beginnings;
my nephew and niece take me to the Vienna Woods.

After the long, cramped flight
I want to go to a swish hotel and dance.

But they scatter me in drifts that cloud their shoes:
for the rest of the day carry me as dust

along streets and houses I loved;
whether they talk of me or not, I'm there,

and neither can bear to wipe me off with a cloth,
until one day their shoes seem quite clean

and they know I have gone.

CONFRONTATION

The crutches give you away:
leg fractured from jumping off a roof
into an adjacent yard
from which you went to burgle my flat.

In your gaze a twitch,
as if a tiny insect
nibbles at the skin below your left eye.
From cupboards and drawers

you have taken my secrets.
Now they break out in your stare.
All else is a locked closet.
The blood on the wall

I've bleached out of my life.
In custody you blamed your mother
for her crippling ways
till you slammed the door in her face.

You had months to think.
Can't hear the rain
drowning out a blackbird's song.
But you can hear my silence:

it is like a tree
cooperating with the fury of a storm.

A GENTLER AGE

In mac and cap he sat on no. 89.
As the wheels rolled
he began to cut.

His scissors meandered with the outside route.
The child in him, fuelled by young boys
with knee-socks and satchels,

shaped a mouse or rabbit,
and, handing over his creation,
watched a puzzled young face

give way to delight:
communion, unspoken, but treasured.
Sometimes, if he thought you worth his while,

the scissors, at a snail's pace,
made the paper grow, then shrink;
performing the ultimate trick: stopping time.

Your questioning eyes – What will it be? –
his presence settling into your slightness.
He knew your stop, reached across

and you unfolded the paper: An angel!
Ran home, almost flying on autumn leaves,
the gift held tight against the wind.

ON THE EDGE

My grandmother looked at the new dress
I was wearing; her index and thumb
shot forward like pincers,

removed a hair from my sleeve
as though it had been a burden on the velvet,
then stroked my arm;

an ease broke through,
she sat me on her knee
and told the story

of how she'd worked at dawn
in her husband's meat-processing plant
and five Russian soldiers

led her to where pigs hung quartered.
While they pointed at the dripping blood
she looked at each in turn,

distantly heard birds still drunk on sleep,
and beyond the confines of the city
the land put out promises on fresh air:

she imagined trees
shot through by wind
when they told her to go back to work.

OBSERVING LOVE AND WAR

From across the village square
the screeching of cats.
Just like humans, the waiter exclaimed,
debating whether they were warring toms
or male and female about to mate.

When it was over I looked at his kind face.
Just like humans, he muttered,
This is my territory – that one yours.
He talked about the Bosnian war.
Burnt houses, and he a boy;

when night drew in, he watched
wrens coming from the deepening
shadows, slipping
into their roosting place
by a splintered door.

He watched for three months.
One evening he sensed the dark unlived in –
the birds did not come.
It was like that time he stared at the crucifix,
the cold in the church turning his legs to stone,

until he felt a tug on his sleeve
and the whisper that it was time to go.

TENDER NIGHT

The air so still
a fullness brushed our empty glasses.

Absent-mindedly you touched your
wedding-ring:
where love began
and ended.

Looking serene in the growing dark,
the living around us taken up
into silence,
you broached the subject of *The Afterlife*:

Would our souls meet,
and if so, in what form?
When I die, you said, *I'll bring my consciousness
before God, and you will be part of it.*

The dark intensified,
but you were still visible
against the backdrop of the wooden fence.

I recall the fullness settling
on our empty glasses,

even now, on a train
watching a young woman in a wheelchair
dressed in white
speak to her boyfriend on her mobile.

Rain soaks the land,
turns to hail, striking the windows –
Stuart, you must come!

Will he? Will she shine in the dark?
Will the moon lift
and lower them
where our cheeks that evening touched?

MARTHA'S REVERIE

They hoist me into the bath
and all I can think of
are elderberries in a large pot:

water, sugar, plums,
cooked until soft,
cooled in the fridge.

My bum itches. I can feel
the underwater breeze as they
lower me and I fart.

Watery brew –
but I cannot think
of the missing ingredient.

His hand on my belly
after we made love.
The joy we had

and somewhere already
the pain of its absence.
Snow. Blizzard.

They spring their youth at me,
make me watch their efficient way
of soaping my skin –

and I glide like a diaphanous shawl,
mistress of my memories
that I can undo in an instant.

They stir up summer.
Sway across my vision with bottles and sponges —
I bear my old age in the belief

that something larger out there
is bearing me.
When the lady from this home

rang the bell of my two up, two down,
I touched the hairline crack
of my ceramic blue-tit:

the coldest day of the year
and she chatted about orioles,
bee-eaters, waxwings.

They rinse me down.
When they blow-dry my hair
something inside me flies

through peepholes of space —
I feel like a child
growing on air. In whirlwind heat

I soar through my life-story —
and there it is:
flour for thickening!

I startle when the sound
is turned off. Ask *why?*
Instead of an answer

there's only that feeling on my lips
as someone combs my hair;
that feeling poised on my cheekbone

as someone puts my curls into place;
that feeling sitting behind my eyelids
as someone shaves bristles off my chin;

that feeling moving underneath my wrinkles
in and out of continents
as someone pats my hand saying *Now you look lovely!*

And I see father's *L* dancing with mother's
o in the sky; plunging,
then climbing into a *v*, allowing the space

to strengthen what lies between them:
the loop of an *e* – the love that writes itself –
and in the fullness of time there was *me*:

swirling up like a leaf from the ground.
How I kicked the other leaves,
scooped them up, and let them drop.

I globed them and clicking my tongue
sent them to all corners of my mind.
They returned, mapping my path.

I skipped over their wine-softness,
their swish and rustle –
how strange that what has died

gives out such glory:
granny knits a rainbow scarf
and mother says *There's always a new beginning*

when you close your eyes.
I smile back that feeling
as when I've eaten all my porridge,

looking at the white glaze
of the empty bowl
with a sense of trust.

BRACELET IN A SHOE

Hidden in the heel of a shoe
it moved with its wearer
from ghetto to cattle-train;
stood still with its wearer
in human waste;
the foot pressing hard on the gold.
The old and sick were taken left,
the young right. The heels
began to crack over time.
She stuffed the bracelet in bits
of stale bread, in freezing water
softened the crumbs to conceal
the small links of chain.
It was the only gold to go into Auschwitz
and come out with its owner.
She wears it to this day:
on her age-spotted skin
each gold link is like the word *love*
that once left her mother's lips;
became a cry, a scream, a soundless plea;
has come back to its original meaning.

TIME

Seeing you arm in arm with your wife
taking slow steps on the rose-lined path
into the wood

I knew this could be the last time;
the illness had shrunk you,
and smiles were hard-fought-for.

Not long ago we chuckled at the impatience
of every child wanting to grow up overnight.
Soon you were deep in the wood.

Then came back from the other side,
back into bright sunlight:
Look, what I've found!

A fossil, where the wood bordered a field,
in dark brown soil that nursed
young seedlings.

A fossil over which a snail
had left a glistening trail.
Your voice filled with new energy

as the find dropped from your hand
into mine. We marvelled at the earth
mixing past, present and future.

Time, you said,
feeling for your wife's arm.
Time. This charitable thought.

THE ANAESTHETIST

All day he anaesthetised patients and now
is late at the Barber Surgeons' Hall
for the Christmas banquet.

Dinner has finished. He tucks into what's left
of the mincemeat-flavoured ice-cream, drinks too much,
staggers past Holbein's Henry VIII into the arms

of the guest speaker who thinks it a laugh
for this resourceful man to cry on his shoulder.
He drinks more and more, wakes up to the

absurdity of his job, is helped from the
floor and into the ritual of raising the "loving cup",
a toast to good health involving three men,

the one in the centre protecting the drinker
with his back (so as not to be stabbed like
King Edward in 10th century Corfe).

He does so, knowing his wish for health
is a mere breath in the wind.
On the train home he slumps into a seat

reserved for a lady who insists he move.
He shuts his eyes like a dog who's heard
it too often from his master. Goes down

into the depths where his ideal,
a young beautiful woman, waits.
But he must not touch, or linger.

He warms to her black-curled hair,
lifts his eyelids as the train draws into his station –
the heavy door swings open –

the platform empty and big as a lake,
he raises his hands as if to receive love –
is wide awake as the dark swallows him up.

20ᵀᴴ JULY 1969

Granny kept the TV on in the next room.
Though off school, I went to bed early,
not wanting to watch the first man
land on the moon.

Pulled the duvet over my head
and underneath explored my own moonscape:
wriggling along eiderdown walls, scaling pillows,
horsehair from the mattress pricking my bottom.

Was it as desolate where the astronauts
disembarked? I fancied *Armstrong* –
the name floated into my near-airtight cocoon
as I simulated the first walk,

the first imprint of feet
on chartless ground.
Looking back at earth
would he know where I was?

Going deeper, the bedclothes' heat
almost asphyxiated me. *No weather on the moon.*
No weather in my bed –
but then came granny's call: *You have missed it!*

Breaking wind, I made my moon collapse
as I dived up for air:
One small step for man, one giant leap for mankind,
I heard it say

and soon granny crept into bed beside mine.
My fingers nestled
in her big warm palm. I waited
until she snored. The streetlight went out

and somewhere the moon
pulsed with cold beauty; first man
collected its dust and sand, my eyes closed,
my hand slipping.

FRIDAY 3 P.M.

Hands lifting from the book
you listen to the Catholic bells
ringing the death of Christ.

A certainty you still possess:
Must bake that cake. –
No – but I repress the word.

How sure you'd been of the ingredients –
but now you would not know whether
to heat the butter or separate the eggs.

The wheelchair holds you in its vice,
the mind a trampoline from which thoughts
jump off, never to return.

I take your hand. The peal of three o'clock.
A death – or do the bells
bring happiness?

You look perplexed.
I too don't know.
Maybe life cannot be measured

by achievement or experience;
that in the end all disappears,
and like you we gaze with an unvoiced question:

You've already baked the cake, I reassure,
Have eaten it as well.
Slowly you let go of my hand.

PRAYING IN SECRET

Pulling out from a drawer
your crocheted throw,
a hand-written notebook
falls into my hands.

In neat letters on the first page:
Pray in secret.
After cleaning it
I spread the throw on the chair.

Patchwork of colours, almost
Mexican. How did you manage
such a large piece
in your small room?

Living alone – no one to help
with layout and pattern.
Balls of intertwined wool
unravelling on the frayed rug.

I sit on your work and imagine
you praying in secret:
time given to peace,
skilled hand quickening the thread.

Imagine you praying
for a brother who never returned from the War,
enough to pay the weekly rent,
kind words from neighbours and friends.

This too is prayer:
the age you lived in so different
touching mine – my idle finger
caught in a hollow between loops.

AMONG RUINS

Where pigeons huddled in wall crevices
and monks prayed for atonement from sins,
she could only think of sex.

Under crumbling pillars where the cold
trained each bone into submission,
she remembered her French knickers

and black-laced corset
at the back of her wardrobe.
She wanted to be seduced

by the man who'd married her.
He walked with a guide-book
past a wandering cat who held each step

like an egg its yolk. The little scrap
of paper in her coat pocket: ... *he gazed
at her naked body and she trembled* –

copied from some romantic fiction.
Even silence spoke in the wind,
ancient trees lifted their secrets

behind tall grass.
He told her about the chanting
monks filled with Christ,

with slow deliberation breathing life
into Latin. She wondered if the angels
collected their Hallelujahs like lucky charms.

At a café she escaped his indifference
by flicking through a magazine.
Look, a nude! She held up the picture.

He looked away. But after paying the bill
kissed her cheek,
cupped her head in his hands

like soothing a child not granted its wish –
and in the sun's glittering pinwheel
drew his fingers from her face.

ECLIPSED MOON

You lie broken in the bed,
your stare a child's
that wants but cannot get.
Hands have lost the touch of love,
fingernails so rough, bones so brittle.

Remember twenty years ago
we willed the clouds to part
for us to see the eclipsed moon.
You fell asleep before it happened.
I too could not stay awake.

It's happening again.
I watch the Earth's shadow
slide over the moon. *Come*, I whisper,
when the event has almost peaked.
And something in you feasts

like a dog on being stroked.
Your frail body moves as if to
embrace what had once been:
your breath clouds my spectacles
and now I cannot see.

I BECAME A FAMOUS ARTIST IN OLD AGE

(based on Carmen Herrera's life-story)

It begins with a black circle.
The colour is singing
like a thrush in spring
welcoming rain.

It deepens into night;
not the cold, impenetrable
pitch-black,
but a warm, blood-like feel.

I live with the black circle
for a while. A time will come
when a shape asks
to be put inside.

I don't know in advance
what it will be. My joints ache
with old age,
but when I begin to paint

I'm like a tree
that spring touches with green.
And I paint a green triangle
into the black circle.

Call it God, or fate –
I've lived for ninety-four years –
the black determined that;
and the green, made up of blue

and yellow – that is the sum of my life:
with each stroke
it grows more vibrant:
alive to the force of the black.

CONTEMPLATION

Unspoken words brush your cheek,
move past the glass of water by your side,
the folded spectacles
towards the mahogany chair catching the sun's

wild dress; the Persian rug holding all the meaning
we strive a lifetime to possess;
the bought, inherited, the given –
each thing like a rare fish on the seabed.

One day all will be displaced, sold, or destroyed,
will make way for someone else's style,
the walls repainted, and silence will guide
the placing of a new object –

but for now, sunlight streaming across your closed eyes,
this delta of light dictates your spatial flight,
soft in-sleep-murmurs
like Chagall to his dream-horse.